I0435076

U.S. Fish and Wildlife Service

Evaluating The Reproductive Success Of Arkansas River Shiner By Assessing Early Life-History Stage Dispersal And Survival At A Landscape Level

Shannon K. Brewer[1]
Timothy B. Grabowski[2]

[1] U.S. Geological Survey, Oklahoma Cooperative Fish and Wildlife Research Unit, Oklahoma State University, Stillwater, OK

[2] U.S. Geological Survey, Texas Cooperative Fish and Wildlife Research Unit, Texas Tech University, Lubbock, TX

Cooperator Science Series # 103

About the Cooperator Science Series:

The Cooperator Science Series was initiated in 2013. Its purpose is to facilitate the archiving and retrieval of research project reports resulting primarily from investigations supported by the U.S. Fish and Wildlife Service (FWS), particularly the Wildlife and Sport Fish Restoration Program. The online format was selected to provide immediate access to science reports for FWS, state and tribal management agencies, the conservation community, and the public at large.

All reports in this series have been subjected to a peer review process consistent with the agencies and entities conducting the research. Authors and/or agencies/institutions providing these reports are solely responsible for their content. The FWS does not provide editorial or technical review of these reports. Comments and other correspondence on reports in this series should be directed to the report authors or agencies/institutions. In most cases, reports published in this series are preliminary to publication, in the current or revised format, in peer reviewed scientific literature. Results and interpretation of data contained within reports may be revised following further peer review or availability of additional data and/or analyses prior to publication in the scientific literature.

The Cooperator Science Series is supported and maintained by the FWS, National Conservation Training Center at Shepherdstown, WV. The series is sequentially numbered with the publication year appended for reference and started with Report No. 101-2013. Various other numbering systems have been used by the FWS for similar, but now discontinued report series. Starting with No. 101 for the current series is intended to avoid any confusion with earlier report numbers.

The use of contracted research agencies and institutions, trade, product, industry or firm names or products or software or models, whether commercially available or not, is for informative purposes only and does not constitute an endorsement by the U.S. Government.

Contractual References:

This document fulfills agreement number F11AP00112. Previously published documents that partially fulfilled any portion of this contract are referenced within, when applicable. (USGS IPDS: IP-046039)

Recommended citation:

Brewer, S. K. and T. B. Grabowski. 2013. Evaluating the reproductive success of Arkansas River shiner by assessing early life-history stage dispersal and survival at a landscape level. U.S. Department of Interior, Fish and Wildlife Service, Cooperator Science Series FWS/CSS-103, Washington, D.C.

For additional copies or information, contact:

Shannon Brewer
U.S. Geological Survey
Oklahoma Cooperative Fish and Wildlife Research Unit
Oklahoma State University
404 Life Sciences West
Stillwater, Oklahoma 74078
Phone: (405) 744-6342
E-mail: shannon.brewer@okstate.edu

EVALUATING THE REPRODUCTIVE SUCCESS OF ARKANSAS RIVER SHINER BY ASSESSING EARLY LIFE-HISTORY STAGE DISPERSAL AND SURVIVAL AT A LANDSCAPE LEVEL (FWS AGREEMENT NUMBER F11AP00112)

Final report to the U.S. Fish and Wildlife Service Great Plains Landscape Conservation Cooperative, May 2013

Shannon K. Brewer

U.S. Geological Survey, Oklahoma Cooperative Fish and Wildlife Research Unit
Oklahoma State University
404 Life Sciences West
Stillwater, Oklahoma 74078
phone: 405-744-6342 | fax: 405-744-5006
e-mail: shannon.brewer@okstate.edu

Timothy B. Grabowski

U.S. Geological Survey, Texas Cooperative Fish and Wildlife Research Unit
Texas Tech University
218 Agricultural Sciences MS 2120
Lubbock, Texas 79409
phone: 806-742-2851 | fax: 806-742-2946
e-mail: t.grabowski@ttu.edu

EXECUTIVE SUMMARY

Reduced to its most fundamental level, the management problem addressed by this project is the basic conflict between the fact that fish need water and the reality that the amount and quality of the water available has been dramatically altered by human activities. For fishes dependent upon specific flows for successful reproduction, the quality and quantity of available water are likely the primary determinants of habitat quality. In many cases, the minimum requirements of water quantity and quality needed to support self-sustaining fish populations are unknown and thus there is no way for resource managers to effectively assess habitat quality and its ability to support fish populations under current or future conditions. The project had two main goals: 1) build a predictive model at the landscape scale to assess the probability of Arkansas River shiner occurrence given a suite of landscape metrics and 2) assess the effects and interactions of environmental factors, e.g., temperature, suspended solids, channel geometry, and flow, on egg buoyancy and early life-history stage survival through laboratory and field experiments. The first goal had one objective- to predict the probability of Arkansas River shiner presence across the entire range under historical and recent environmental conditions and identify significant landscape metrics relating to those distributional changes. The second goal had three objectives- 1) assess the effects of temperature, salinity, and suspended solids on early life stages of Arkansas River shiner, 2) determine the efficiency of the Moore Egg Collector, a gear commonly used to collect drifting eggs of Arkansas River shiner and other members of the pelagic broadcast spawning guild, and 3) assess the influence of stream geomorphology on Arkansas River shiner egg transport.

Several final products have been submitted to U.S. Fish and Wildlife Service in addition to this final report. The single objective identified in the first project goal was completed and is In Press in Global Change Biology (http://onlinelibrary.wiley.com/doi/10.1111/gcb.12329/pdf). The second project goal had three objectives and the first two objectives were completed prior to this report: Objective one was completed as a Master's thesis and objective two was completed and published in the North American Journal of Fisheries Management (DOI:10.1080/02755947.2012.741557).

The full citation to each product is listed below:

Mueller, J. 2013. Effects of temperature, salinity, and suspended solids on the early life history stages of Arkansas River shiner. MS Thesis, Texas Tech University, Lubbock.

Worthington, T.A., S.K. Brewer, T.B. Grabowski, and J. Mueller. In Press. Backcasting the decline of a vulnerable Great Plains reproductive ecotype: Identifying threats and conservation priorities. Global Change Biology doi: 10.1111/gcb.12329.

Worthington, T.A., S.K. Brewer, T.B. Grabowski, and J. Mueller. 2013. Evaluating the sampling efficiency of the Moore egg collector. North American Journal of Fisheries Management 33:79–88.

The third and final objective has not yet been published and the results are included in this report with a summary below.

Habitat fragmentation and flow regulation are significant factors related to the decline and extinction of freshwater biota. Pelagic broadcast-spawning cyprinids represent a threatened guild of fishes that require moving water and some length of stream to complete their life cycle. However, it is unknown how discharge and habitat features interact at multiple spatial scales to alter the transport of semi-buoyant fish eggs. Our objective was to assess the relationship between downstream drift of semi-buoyant egg surrogates (beads) and discharge and habitat complexity. We released a known quantity of beads at seven locations on the North Canadian and Canadian rivers. Habitat complexity was assessed by calculating width: depth ratios at each site, and several habitat metrics determined from aerial photographs analyses. We quantified the capture of beads using two or three egg collectors at each site. Median time of egg capture was significantly and negatively related to site discharge. Extent of the sampling period at each site was significantly and negatively related to site discharge and habitat patch dispersion. Our results highlight the role of discharge in driving transport times but also the dispersion of habitat patches across the landscape. Higher dispersion of habitat patches related to increased retention of beads

3

within the river. The management implications are important given the high demands for water and the importance of drift for many threatened Great Plains species. These results could be used to target restoration activities or prioritize water use to create and maintain habitat complexity within large, fragmented river systems.

Background

Across all biomes, habitat fragmentation, loss and degradation are frequently cited as main causes of species decline and extinction (Bascompte and Sole, 1996; Doak, 1995; Ehrlich, 1995; Fahrig, 2002). In freshwater ecosystems, fragmentation and flow regulation have severely degraded many of the world's rivers (Revenga et al., 2000; Nilsson et al., 2005). River regulation typically results in reduced habitat heterogeneity, a loss in lateral and longitudinal connectivity (Mann, 1988; Haslam, 1990), and an altered flow regime (Lytle and Poff, 2004). The impact of these changes to the natural functioning of river systems are often manifested in reduced diversity (Gorman and Karr, 1978; Gehrke et al., 1995), biomass and density (Cowx et al., 1986; Penczak, 1995; Pilcher et al., 2004) of aquatic organisms.

Within the United States, 85% of large rivers are impacted by the presence of barriers (Hughes et al., 2005), resulting in the natural continuum being divided into poorly connected fragments (see Perkin and Gido, 2011). This degradation of natural habitat, alongside other factors, has resulted in approximately 40% of fish species in continental North American being considered imperilled (Jelks et al., 2008). In the Great Plains, there has been a marked decline in the native fish fauna over the preceding 50 years, with many species that exhibit unique life-history adaptations showing reductions in both distribution and abundance (Gido et al., 2010). The rivers of the Great Plains are subject to extremes in physicochemical conditions (Matthews, 1987), with the timing of high and low flow events subject to extensive temporal variability (Poff, 1996). Under such conditions, it has been suggested that aquatic organisms may undertake bet-hedging strategies as part of their life history (Lytle and Poff, 2004). Pelagic broadcast-spawning cyprinids (pelagophils) are a reproductive guild of small minnows historically abundant in rivers of the Great Plains (Williams & Bonner, 2006; Hoagstrom et al., 2011; Perkins & Gido, 2011). These species, which include the federally threatened Arkansas River shiner *Notropis girardi* produce eggs that achieve semi-buoyancy soon after fertilization, but require water movement to remain in suspension (Moore, 1944; Platania and Altenbach 1998, Dudley and Platania 1999). Members of this reproductive guild also display fractional or extended spawning (Fausch and Bestgen, 1997), a potential mechanism to cope with variability in the timing of high-flow events. To reach a free-swimming stage, the eggs and larvae, ichthyoplankton, need to remain in suspension for 3-5 days (Moore, 1944; Platania and

Altenbach 1998), and therefore require extensive sections of free-flowing river (Dudley and Platania 2007; Perkin and Gido, 2011).

This life history is likely to render pelagophils particularly sensitive to river fragmentation (Hoagstrom et al., 2011). The construction of large reservoirs throughout the Great Plains has dramatically altered the timing and magnitude of high-flow events (Limbird, 1993; Bonner and Wilde, 2002). Loss of high flows potentially disrupts spawning cues (see Moore, 1944), reduces water available to maintain downstream movement of eggs and larvae (Platania and Altenbach 1998), and interrupts channel-forming processes. The reduction in unfragmented channel sections may result in the ichthyoplankton being washed into unsuitable habitats such as reservoirs where they may smother in sediment or be subjected to increased predation risk (Platania and Altenbach 1998). Pelagic broadcast spawners are thought to undertake upstream migrations to recolonize areas following downstream drift (see Platania and Altenbach, 1998; Bonner, 2000), these movements could be truncated due to the presence of large dams (e.g., Hoagstrom et al., 2010).

Several studies have examined egg transport at catchment scales for Great Plains pelagic broadcast spawning cyprinids (e.g., Dudley and Platania, 2007; Medley et al., 2007; Widmer et al., 2012); however, little research has quantified the role of channel complexity at a more local scale on the downstream movement of semi-buoyant fish eggs. The aim of this study was to examine how flow and habitat heterogeneity impact the movement rate of artificial fish eggs in two Great Plains rivers that form part of the Arkansas River shiner's historical distribution (see previous section of this report). We hypothesized that in reaches with greater habitat complexity the downstream egg movement rate will be decreased, when compared to more homogenous reaches. This has important implications for the conservation of pelagic spawning cyprinids, as the length of river required to complete development to the free swimming larvae stage would be reduced in areas of higher habitat complexity.

Materials and Methods

Habitat Complexity

Experiments were completed on the Canadian and North Canadian rivers, Oklahoma to assess the relation between habitat complexity and egg transport time. Prior to field sampling, habitat structure of 13 potential sites was assessed using FRAGSTATS version 4.0, which analyzes landscape spatial patterns (McGarigal et al., 2012). Thirteen sites were selected from the U.S. Fish and Wildlife Service survey locations and represented sections where Arkansas River shiner had been recorded between 2007 and 2009 (Canadian River, n = 11) and where the species was absent during surveys in 2007 (North Canadian River, n = 2; D. Fenner, personal communication; Figure 1).

We downloaded the most recent aerial photographs (2010) of the thirteen sites (The Geospatial Data Gateway (GDG), http://datagateway.nrcs.usda.gov/GDGHome.aspx) and displayed them in ArcMap 9.3 (ESRI, Redlands, CA, USA). A 1000-m section of the channel upstream of each survey site was selected and the boundary of the channel, marked by a continuous vegetation edge, was delineated. This polygon was used to clip the area of interest from band 1 of the aerial photograph. The reclassify tool in ArcGIS was used to create a new raster layer by splitting band 1 into four habitat categories representing deep water (sand not visible), shallow water (sand visible), exposed sand and vegetation (Figure 2). The newly created layer was visually inspected for consistency with the original aerial photograph and areas of incongruence were manually corrected.

We opened the thirteen raster files in FRAGSTATS and calculated the area of each habitat category as a percentage of the overall landscape, and three landscape metrics: (1) total landscape area, (2) mean 'shape index' (the complexity of patch shapes in comparison to a square) and (3) mean 'contagion index' (level to which patches are dispersed across the landscape; O'Neill et al., 1988). The 13 sites were then ranked based on the three landscape metrics to provide an overall score of habitat complexity and integrity (Table 1). It was hypothesized that sites with a greater total landscape area were likely to represent wide shallow sections that had not been subject to high levels of channel modification, and that sites with a higher shape index and lower contagion index would be more heterogeneous. From this overall ranking, five sites on the Canadian River were selected to represent a range of the habitat scores, alongside both sites from the North Canadian River, due to the species being absent from recent surveys on that river. However, upon field inspection, the downstream site on the North Canadian River (Ft. Supply) (at ~ 0.42 m^3s^{-1}) was not a useable site due to the quantity and density of vegetation that had grown in the river channel. The Ft. Supply location was replaced by another site on the North Canadian River at El Reno. The El Reno site provides an interesting contrast between the other North Canadian site (Laverne) and the South Canadian sites, being intermediate in terms of channel size (width) and discharge. Further, one site on the South Canadian (Norman) was moved ~ 1km downstream due to difficulties obtaining access. The same FRAGSTATS procedure was undertaken for the new Norman location and the El Reno replacement site (Table 1).

Aerial photograph habitat classifications were validated in the field at each site. We randomly generated 25 points using ArcGIS and navigated to each of these points using a Trimble GeoXH differential global positioning system (DGPS) (sub meter accuracy; Trimble Navigation Limited, Sunnyvale, California, USA). We assessed habitat classification at each point: sand, water (shallow and deep combined) or vegetation. At our replacement site on the North Canadian River, we haphazardly chose 25 points and classified the habitat, which we later verified using the aerial photograph. Predictions from the aerial photographs where then compared to the field measurements and the percentage of correctly assigned categories assessed.

Egg Transport Time

Transport time was assessed by releasing a known quantity of egg surrogates (gellan beads) and recording the temporal distribution of recaptures. Gellan beads (Technology Flavors and Fragrances, Inc., Amityville, New York) have similar physical properties including shape and specific gravity to the eggs of pelagic broadcast spawning cyprinids (Medley et al., 2007; Widmer et al., 2012). At each sampling site, 3,450 g of gellan beads were released, equating to approximately 100,000 (95% CI: 98,690 – 101,050) beads. The 95% confidence interval for the weight of a single bead was calculated by weighing 52 batches of 1,000 beads to the nearest 0.01 g. Prior to weighing, the gellan beads were rinsed to remove excess syrup used as preservative during storage. Gellan beads were soaked in freshwater for a minimum of 24 hrs prior to release (Reinert et al., 2004) to more closely match the specific gravity of Arkansas River shiner eggs (Dudley and Platania, 1999).

Experiments took place in March 2013. The gellan beads were recaptured using Moore Egg Collectors (MECs) (see Worthington et al., 2013 for a complete description). Briefly, the MEC is a device designed for the collection of semi-buoyant fish eggs, which is secured in the upper portion of the water column (Altenbach et al., 2000). The open upstream end of the MEC allows floating propagules to enter the device from where they are swept up a mesh screen at the water-air interface. For the five sites initially assessed for habitat complexity, the downstream location of the MECs and the upstream release point of the gellan beads were identified using ArcGIS by delineating the middle 500-m of the 1000-m assessment section. We located the downstream and upstream site extent using a DGPS. For the two replacement sites, a suitable deployment location for the MECs was selected near the site access and the release point measured 500-m upstream. At each site, depending on channel width, two or three MECs were deployed in areas of concentrated flow as laboratory studies indicated the surrogate fish eggs are highly spatially aggregated and are therefore likely to move in areas of concentrated discharge (Worthington et al., 2013). The MECs were placed in parallel facing the direction of flow with the opening of the box submerged just below the waterline. The gellan beads were released at single point, in an area of bulk flow, 500-m upstream from the MECs. The number of beads captured every minute per MEC was recorded until a period of 5 consecutive minutes of no captures occurred.

Discharge and geomorphology were assessed at each site. We examined variability in fluvial geometry between sampling sites by measuring five width-to-depth ratios (Gordon et al., 1992) at each site. Width:depth was measured at five randomly selected transects, stratified every 100-m through the study site. At each transect, depth was measured every 1-m across the channel. Discharge was measured at one or more transects at each site using the velocity-area method (Gordon et al., 1992). Discharge was also assessed using gage measurements at the time of the bead release from the closest U.S. Geological Survey (USGS) gage on the same river (Gage numbers: 07229200, 07228500, 07239500, 07237500, http://waterdata.usgs.gov/usa/nwis/rt).

Statistical Analyses

Transport time was assessed by comparing the temporal distributions of gellan bead captures between sites. Bead captures from the individual MECs at each site were combined to produce a site measure and plotted as a cumulative distribution function. Two separate models were constructed to evaluate the median capture time (the time at which 50% of gellan beads had been captured) and the sampling period (the time period between which 2.5% to 97.5% of gellan beads were captured). Times were calculated in minutes and decimal seconds by interpolating between the two points. Initial explanatory variables were the four metrics calculated using FRAGSTATS, the mean of the site width-to-depth ratios, site discharge, and the USGS gage discharge values. Pearson product-moment correlations revealed high levels of colinearity between site discharge and width-to-depth ratio ($r = 0.87$, $n = 7$, $P = 0.01$), total site area ($r = 0.98$, $n = 7$, $P < 0.001$) and USGS gage discharge ($r = 0.95$, $n = 7$, $P < 0.001$). Site discharge was predicted to be the primary factor determining downstream drift; therefore this variable was selected for use in the models. The vegetation category was relatively uncommon ($< 9\ \%$) in the aerial photographs so it was therefore removed from the analysis. The percentage of water at a site (shallow and deep combined) was also omitted because it was significantly correlated with the percentage of sand ($r = -0.96$, $n = 7$, $P < 0.001$). The final set of four explanatory variables was: percentage of sand at a site, mean shape index, mean contagion index and site discharge.

The relationship between the two dependent variables, median capture time and sampling period, and the four explanatory variables was modelled using ordinary least squares regression models, constructed using SPSS (SPSS 20.0.0, IBM Corp). Predictor selection was carried out using a combination of a hierarchical framework and forward entry method. Discharge was entered first because we expected it to most heavily influence drift of the beads. The remaining three variables were then sequentially entered into the model and improvements in model fit were assessed after each variable was entered. Predictors were retained in the model if they were significantly related to the dependent variable ($\alpha < 0.05$). Data were transformed (natural log) if examination of standardized residuals and Cook's distance measure (Weisberg, 1982) suggested model assumptions were violated. If assumptions were still violated, bootstrapping was used (1,000 iterations) to provide robust confidence intervals of the parameter β values (Field, 2009).

Results

Habitat Complexity

There was considerable variation in the habitat metrics calculated using FRAGSTATS (Table 1). Site total area was particularly variable but followed a fairly consistent pattern, with total area increasing from upstream to downstream and those sites on the North Canadian having a smaller total area than those on the Canadian River. The complexity of habitat patch shape was greatest at Bridgeport, whereas El Reno had the highest contagion index score. Discounting the two replacement sites; overall, Wanette was predicted as having the most heterogeneous habitat ranking high in both total area and contagion index, whereas Purcell ranked low for the shape index and contagion index metrics (Table 1). Field validation showed reasonable agreement in habitat categories assigned from the aerial photographs. Across the seven sites, 73% (range: 64% - 84%) of 25 points were correctly assigned to a habitat category.

Egg Transport

Median capture time was remarkably similar for the Canadian River sites, ranging from 15 to 21 minutes (Table 2). For the North Canadian sites, the median time to capture at the El Reno site was closer to those in the Canadian River (~32 minutes), whereas Laverne was significantly greater at almost 2 hours (Table 2). Median capture time and sampling period were highly correlated ($r = 0.96$, $n = 7$, $P = 0.01$). Further examination suggested the relationship was overly influenced by the Laverne point, this point was removed and no relationship between median capture time and sampling period was apparent ($r = 0.06$, $n = 6$, $P = 0.90$). Unlike median capture time, sampling period was far more variable ranging from 5 to 52 minutes for the Canadian River sites. Sampling period was shortest at Bridgeport with 95% of gellan beads being captured within 5 minutes, compared to approximately 200 minutes at Laverne.

Median capture time was significantly ($F_{5, 6} = 8.53$, $P = 0.033$) and negatively related to site discharge ($t = -2.92$, $P = 0.033$), with the model explaining 63% of the observed variance (Figure 3). Concern of the relative influence of the Laverne point and violation of the assumption of linearity rendered examination of the bootstrapped estimated of the discharge predictors necessary. These bootstrapped confident intervals (CI) of the discharge predictor confirmed the negative trend in the relationship between discharge and median capture time $\beta = -0.21$ (95% CI: $-0.35 – -0.05$).

Sampling period was significantly ($F_{4, 6} = 38.07$, P = 0.002) and negatively related to two predictor variables, site discharge (t = -7.52, P = 0.002) and contagion index (t = -7.35, P = 0.002), with the model explaining 95% of the observed variance. Suggested violation of the assumptions of heteroscedasticity and nonlinearity required examination of the bootstrapped predictor estimates. These bootstrapped confident intervals (CI) confirmed the negative trends in the relationship between the predictor variables and sampling period: discharge $\beta = -0.44$ (95% CI: $-0.57 – -0.40$), contagion index $\beta = -0.13$ (95% CI: $-0.23 – -0.12$).

Discussion and Conclusions

The rivers and streams of the Great Plains were historically characterized by predominately sandy substrate and wide braided channels (Matthews, 1988). The natural flow regime was extremely variable and typified by extreme flood and drought periods (Dodds et al., 2004). Channelization, impoundments, water abstraction and land-use change has greatly impacted the functioning of these rivers (Dodds et al., 2004). Increasing groundwater pumping and incidence of drought has resulted in smaller streams being absent of water for extended periods, while main river channels are often restricted to a simple, narrow thalweg (Woods et al., 2005). Dam construction has resulted in loss flow regime variability, transforming these dynamic rivers into more static systems (Julian et al., 2011). These changes to the natural river functioning are thought to have driven the decline and extinction of many Great Plains endemic fishes (Rabeni, 1996; Hoagstrom et al., 2011). Fragmentation (Perkin and Gido, 2011), and altered flow regimes (Hughes et al., 2005) have rendered the reproductive guild of pelagic broadcast spawning cyprinids particularly vulnerable (Warren et al., 2000; Jelks et al., 2008). A paradigm shift has been advocated for the conservation of these cyprinids, which suggests attempting to identify the life-stages limiting population persistence (Wilde and Durham, 2008) and a greater focus on early life stages (Durham and Wilde, 2009).

Studies of the early life stages of pelagic broadcast spawning, cyprinids species, have examined reproductive strategies (Platania and Altenbach, 1998), population dynamics (Hoagstrom et al., 2008; Wilde and Durham, 2008; Durham and Wilde, 2009), and reproductive season (Taylor and Miller, 1990; Durham and Wilde, 2005, 2006). Flow regime is often the critical determinant structuring the factor of interest. A number of abiotic and biotic factors influence the drift dynamics of fish (Harvey, 1991; Johnston et al., 1995) and invertebrates (Brittain and Eikeland, 1988), with passive downstream migration greater at higher discharges (Pavlov, 1994; Jiang et al., 2010). Moore (1944) first described the downstream drift of the Arkansas River shiner's semi-buoyant pelagic eggs and proposed a relationship between elevated discharge and the onset of spawning. Our study similarly highlights the role of river discharge in driving the timing of the peak in gellan bead catches. The sites with higher discharges on the Canadian River had a greatly reduced median time to peak gellan bead captures compared to those in the North Canadian where flow was much lower. Transport velocities in our study were lower than those reported in other studies (0.7 m/s: Dudley and Platania, 2007; 0.57 – 1.07 m/s: Widmer et al., 2012); however, the direction of the response is consistent with experiments using passively drifting fish egg surrogates in the Rio Grande and Pecos rivers, where transport time was highly positively correlated to river discharge (Dudley and Platania, 2007).

Although the timing of peak gellan bead captures was driven by discharge independently, the length of sampling period was also related to habitat complexity, in this case the dispersion and interspersion of habitat patches within the landscape (O'Neill et al., 1988). There was high variation between sites in the length of time required to capture the bulk of the gellan beads. Sample period variation was also high among the Canadian River sites and had little relationship to the timing of the peak captures. As discharge and the contagion index increased, the length of time taken to capture the majority of the beads decreased. A lower contagion score suggests a landscape consisting of multiple small and dispersed habitat patches (McGarigal et al., 2012). Within the context of the Great Plains rivers, lower scores would equate to reaches with interspersed areas of shallow and deep water and in channel features such as sandbars and islands. Our results support those of Bond et al. (2000) who suggested that the spatial arrangement of patches is important in structuring the downstream dispersal of passive drifting particles. For pelagic broadcast spawning cyprinids, increased habitat complexity has been suggested to reduce downstream transport distance of the ichtyoplankton stage (e.g. Dudley and Platania, 2007; Medley et al., 2007). Dudley and Platania (2007) stated that transport velocities were greatest in those reaches of the Pecos and Rio Grande rivers described as having narrow and incised channels. They suggested that in sections with wider and more braided channel morphology, slower transport rates would allow more time for ichtyoplankton to reach the free-swimming stage (Dudley and Platania, 2007). The link between discharge and habitat complexity has also been proposed by Medley et al. (2007; see also Widmer et al., 2012); although they suggested that as discharge increases a greater proportion of beads would be retained in upstream reaches due to increased lateral connectivity and channel storage. However a critique and re-analysis of the Medley et al. (2007) approach indicated a number of methodological uncertainties and suggested the relationship between width to depth ratio and retention was 'weak' (Zymonas and Propst, 2009).

This study highlights the joint roles of hydrology and geomorphology in influencing the distribution of downstream drifting gellan beads and by extension, the eggs of pelagic broadcast spawning cyprinids. Discharge appears to determine the timing of peak captures, while discharge and habitat complexity in tandem influence the retention of beads within a reach (Figure 4). At very low discharges, gellan beads or fish eggs are likely to fall out of suspension (see Platania and Altenbach 1998; Mueller, 2013). At discharge levels sufficient to allow downstream transport but where particles travel low in water column, gellan beads appear to be more influenced by microhabitat features such as ridges in the sand substrate (e.g., Laverne site, pers. obs.). As discharge increases, gellan beads are retained higher in the water column (Worthington et al., 2013) and timing of peaks at a set distance downstream are likely to be reduced. In reaches with low habitat complexity, discharge was the controlling factor (e.g., El Reno, Bridgeport); however, sections with greater complexity may serve to retain a larger portion of particles in upstream areas (e.g., Wanette, Taloga). High discharges during flood events may transport particles considerable distances downstream, although a positive feedback mechanism may occur whereby lateral connectivity with the floodplain is increased allowing access to low-velocity habitats and thus retaining greater numbers of eggs upstream (Medley et al., 2007; Widmer et al., 2012).

Our research demonstrates the link between downstream movement of gellan beads, discharge and habitat complexity; however, several factors pertinent to the persistence of populations of pelagic broadcast spawning cyprinids were not included in our models. How does individual egg behavior effect downstream transport distance? All eggs are not created equal. Dudley and Platania (1999) showed small levels of variation in the specific gravity (SG) of pelagic broadcast spawning cyprinids eggs (SG = 1.00589 ± 0.00011). It is therefore likely that

14

individual eggs will respond to the same stimulus differently. Critically, the use of egg surrogates makes it impossible to elucidate the link between downstream drift dynamics and ichtyoplankton survival. The use of gellan beads is driven by the logistics of obtaining large quantities of eggs without impacting populations of threatened species (Reinert et al., 2004). The release of semi-buoyant eggs is thought to render them less vulnerable to suffocation or abrasion by the sand substrate of the river (Bestgen et al., 1989), thus a certain water velocity is required to keep the eggs in suspension (Worthington et al., 2013). However, the exact relationship between contact with the substrate and egg viability is unknown. This has important implications for understanding the river fragment length required for ichtyoplankton to reach the free-swimming stage (e.g., Platania and Altenbach, 1998; Perkin and Gido, 2011). Other factors are also known to affect egg behavior. For example, median buoyancy is negatively correlated with temperature and positively correlated with total suspended solids (Mueller, 2013). Future studies addressing the long-term viability of eggs retained in low-velocity areas (Widmer et al., 2012) would allow more robust calculations of channel length needed to sustain populations, although tracking such small particles over great distances would be extremely challenging and likely require a combination of laboratory, field and modeling approaches.

Our results highlight how disturbance of the natural functioning of river systems and the balance between hydrologic and geomorphologic processes is likely to have contributed to the decline of species such as Arkansas River shiner. Anthropogenic activities have altered the natural flow regime and reduced geomorphic complexity of rivers, potentially increasing the length of channel required for ichthyoplankton to reach the free-swimming stage (Dudley and Platania, 2007). Reservoir construction has fragmented the river network reducing the available suitable habitat and increasing the risk of predation (Luttrell et al., 1999; Quist et al., 2004). Possible management options for species such as Arkansas River shiner include restoring components of the natural flow regime (Dudley and Platania, 2007) and maintaining perennial base flows (Hoagstom et al., 2008), which may potentially re-establish channel forming processes (Poff et al., 1997). Where appropriate, habitat restoration could enhance habitat complexity and connectivity, thereby increasing egg retention (Widmer et al., 2012). Removal of major impoundments within the Arkansas River shiner's former range is not feasible; however, we suggest any future reservoir development or increased storage within existing reservoirs avoid key refugia that currently support vulnerable Great Plains species (Hoagstom et al., 2011; Worthington et al. In press).

Acknowledgements

This research is a contribution of the Oklahoma Cooperative Fish and Wildlife Research Unit (U.S. Geological Survey, Oklahoma Department of Wildlife Conservation, Oklahoma State University, and Wildlife Management Institute cooperating). Funding was provided by the U.S. Fish and Wildlife Service, Great Plains Landscape Conservation Cooperative (U.S. Fish and Wildlife Service agreement F11AP00112). Any use of trade, firm, or product names is for descriptive purposes and does not imply endorsement by the U.S. Government. We thank Mark Gregory, Oklahoma State University for GIS assistance. We also thank B. Brown, N. Farless, and R. Mollenhauer for field assistance; C. Jennings for providing gellan beads; and D. Fenner for technical and logistical assistance. Tom Kwak and Dan Shoup provided helpful comments on earlier drafts of the report.

References

Altenbach CS, Dudley RK, Platania SP. 2000. A new device for collecting drifting semibuoyant fish eggs. *Transactions of the American Fisheries Society* **129**: 296-300. DOI: 10.1577/1548-8659(2000)129<0296:ANDFCD>2.0.CO;2.

Bascompte J, Solé RV. 1996. Habitat fragmentation and extinction thresholds in spatially explicit models. *Journal of Animal Ecology* **65**: 465-473. DOI: 10.2307/5781.

Bestgen KR, Platania SP, Brooks JE, Propst DL. 1989. Dispersal and life history traits of *Notropis girardi* (Cypriniformes: Cyprinidae), introduced into the Pecos River, New Mexico. *The American Midland Naturalist* **122**: 228-235.

Bond NR, Perry GLW, Downes BJ. 2000. Dispersal of organisms in a patchy stream environment under different settlement scenarios. *Journal of Animal Ecology* **69**: 608-619. DOI: 10.1046/j.1365-2656.2000.00420.x.

Bonner TH. 2000. Life history and reproductive ecology of the Arkansas River shiner and peppered chub in the Canadian River, Texas and New Mexico. *Ph.D. Thesis*, Texas Tech University, 147pp.

Bonner TH, Wilde GR. 2002. Effects of turbidity on prey consumption by prairie stream fishes. *Transactions of the American Fisheries Society* **131**: 1203-1208. DOI: 10.1577/1548-8659(2002)131<1203:EOTOPC>2.0.CO;2.

Brittain JE, Eikeland TJ. 1988. Invertebrate drift - a review. *Hydrobiologia* **166**: 77-93. DOI: 10.1007/BF00017485.

Cook RD, Weisberg S. 1982 *Residuals and Influence in Regression*. Chapman and Hall: New York, USA.

Doak DF. 1995. Source-sink models and the problem of habitat degradation: general models and applications to the Yellowstone grizzly. *Conservation Biology* **9**: 1370-1379. DOI: 10.1046/j.1523-1739.1995.09061370.x.

Dudley RK, Platania SP. 1999. Imitating the physical properties of drifting semibuoyant fish (Cyprinidae) eggs with artificial eggs. *Journal of Freshwater Ecology* **14**: 423-430. DOI: 10.1080/02705060.1999.9663700.

Dudley RK, Platania SP. 2007. Flow regulation and fragmentation imperil pelagic-spawning riverine fishes. *Ecological Applications* **17**: 2074-2086. DOI: 10.1890/06-1252.1

Fahrig L. 2002. Effect of habitat fragmentation on the extinction threshold: A synthesis. *Ecological Applications* **12**: 346-353. DOI: 10.1890/1051-0761(2002)012[0346:EOHFOT]2.0.CO;2.

Fausch KD, Bestgen KR. 1997. Ecology of fishes indigenous to the central and southwestern Great Plains. In *Ecology and Conservation of Great Plains Vertebrates. Ecological Studies 125,* Knopf FL, Samson FB (eds). Springer-Verlag: New York, USA; 131-166.

Field A. 2009. *Discovering Statistics Using SPSS, 3rd Edition.* SAGE Publication Ltd.: London

Gido KB, Dodds WK, Eberle ME. 2010. Retrospective analysis of fish community change during a half-century of landuse and streamflow changes. *Journal of the North American Benthological Society* **29**: 970-987. DOI: 10.1899/09-116.1

Gordon ND, McMahon TA, Finlayson BL. 2004. *Stream Hydrology: An Introduction for Ecologists.* John Wiley & Sons: Chichester, UK.

Harvey BC. 1991. Interaction of abiotic and biotic factors influences larval fish survival in an Oklahoma stream. *Canadian Journal of Fisheries and Aquatic Sciences* **48**: 1476-1480. DOI: 10.1139/f91-175.

Hoagstrom CW, Brooks JE, Davenport SR. 2008. Spatiotemporal population trends of *Notropis simus pecosensis* in relation to habitat conditions and the annual flow regime of the Pecos

River, 1992–2005. *Copeia* **2008**: 5–15. DOI: 10.1643/CE-07-002

Hoagstrom CW, Brooks JE, Davenport SR. 2011. A large-scale conservation perspective

considering endemic fishes of the North American plains. *Biological Conservation* **144**:

21-34. DOI: 10.1016/j.biocon.2010.07.015.

Hughes RM, Rinne JN, Calamusso B. 2005. Introduction to historical changes in 16 large river

fish assemblages of the Americas. In *Historical Changes in Large River Fish*

Assemblages of the Americas, Rinne JN, Hughes RM, Calamusso B (eds). American

Fisheries Society: Bethesda, Maryland, USA; 1-12.

Jelks HL, Walsh SJ, Burkhead NM, Contreras-Balderas S, Diaz-Pardo E, Hendrickson DA,

Lyons J, Mandrak NE, McCormick F, Nelson JS, Platania SP, Porter BA, Renaud CB,

Schmitter-Soto JJ, Taylor EB, Warren ML. 2008. Conservation status of imperiled North

American freshwater and diadromous fishes. *Fisheries* **33**: 372-407. DOI: 10.1577/1548-

8446-33.8.372.

Jiang W, Liu H-Z, Duan Z-H, Cao W-X. 2010. Seasonal variation in drifting eggs and larvae in

the Upper Yangtze, China. *Zoological Science* **27**: 402-409. DOI: 10.2108/zsj.27.402.

Johnston TA, Gaboury MN, Janusz RA, Janusz LR. 1995. Larval fish drift in the Valley River,

Manitoba: influence of abiotic and biotic factors, and relationships with future year-class

strengths. *Canadian Journal of Fisheries and Aquatic Sciences* **52**: 2423-2431. DOI:

10.1139/f95-833.

Limbird RL. 1993. The Arkansas River: a changing river. In *Restoration Planning for Rivers of*

the Mississippi River Ecosystem, Hesse LW, Stalnaker CB, Benson NB, Zuboy JR (eds).

National Biological Survey: Washington, D.C., USA; 81–94.

Luttrell GR, Echelle AA, Fisher WL, Eisenhour DJ. 1999. Declining status of two species of the *Macrhybopsis aestivalis* complex (Teleostei: Cyprinidae) in the Arkansas River Basin and related effects of reservoirs as barriers to dispersal. *Copeia* **1999**: 981-989.

Lytle DA, Poff NL. 2004. Adaptation to natural flow regimes. *Trends in Ecology & Evolution* **19**: 94-100. DOI: 10.1016/j.tree.2003.10.002.

Matthews WJ. 1988. North American prairie streams as systems for ecological study. *Journal of the North American Benthological Society* **7**: 387-409.

McGarigal K, Cushman SA, Ene E. 2012. *FRAGSTATS v4: Spatial Pattern Analysis Program for Categorical and Continuous Maps.* University of Massachusetts: Amherst, Massachusetts, USA.

Medley CN, Kehmeier JW, Myers OB, Valdez RA. 2007. Simulated transport and retention of pelagic fish eggs during an irrigation release in the Pecos River, New Mexico. *Journal of Freshwater Ecology* **22**: 499-513. DOI: 10.1080/02705060.2007.9664180.

Moore GA. 1944. Notes on the early life history of *Notropis girardi. Copeia* **1944**: 209-214.

Mueller J. 2013. Effects of temperature, salinity, and suspended solids on the early life history stages of Arkansas River Shiner. *MSc Thesis*, Texas Tech University, 48pp.

O'Neill RV, Krummel JR, Gardner RH, Sugihara G, Jackson B, DeAngelis DL, Milne BT, Turner MG, Zygmunt B, Christensen SW, Dale VH, Graham RL. 1988. Indices of landscape pattern. *Landscape Ecology* **1**: 153-162. DOI: 10.1007/bf00162741.

Pavlov DS. 1994. The downstream migration of young fishes in rivers:mechanisms and distribution. *Folia Zoologica* **43**: 193-208.

Perkin JS, Gido KB. 2011. Stream fragmentation thresholds for a reproductive guild of Great Plains fishes. *Fisheries* **36**: 371-383. DOI: 10.1080/03632415.2011.597666.

Platania SP, Altenbach CS. 1998. Reproductive strategies and egg types of seven Rio Grande

    Basin cyprinids. *Copeia* **1998**: 559-569.

Poff N. 1996. A hydrogeography of unregulated streams in the United States and an examination

    of scale-dependence in some hydrological descriptors. *Freshwater Biology* **36**: 71-79.

    DOI: 10.1046/j.1365-2427.1996.00073.x.

Poff NL, Allan JD, Bain MB, Karr JR, Prestegaard KL, Richter BD, Sparks RE, Stromberg JC.

    1997. The natural flow regime. *BioScience* **47**: 769-784. DOI: 10.2307/1313099.

Quist MC, Hubert WA, Rahel FJ. 2004. Relations among habitat characteristics, exotic species,

    and turbid-river cyprinids in the Missouri River drainage of Wyoming. *Transactions of*

    the American Fisheries Society **133**: 727-742. DOI: 10.1577/T03-124.1.

Reinert TR, Will TA, Jennings CA, Davin WT. 2004. Use of egg surrogates to estimate sampling

    efficiency of striped bass eggs in the Savannah River. *North American Journal of*

    Fisheries Management **24**: 704-710. DOI: 10.1577/m02-186.1.

Widmer A, Fluder J, Kehmeier J, Medley C, Valdez R. 2012. Drift and retention of pelagic

    spawning minnow eggs in a regulated river. *River Research and Applications* **28**: 192-

    203. DOI: 10.1002/rra.1454.

Williams CS, Bonner TH. 2006. Habitat associations, life history and diet of the Sabine shiner

    Notropis sabinae in an east Texas drainage. *The American Midland Naturalist* **155**: 84-

    102. DOI: 10.1674/0003-0031(2006)155[0084:halhad]2.0.co;2.

Worthington TA, Brewer SK, Grabowski TB, Mueller J. 2013. Sampling efficiency of the Moore

    egg collector. *North American Journal of Fisheries Management* **33**: 79-88. DOI:

    10.1080/02755947.2012.741557.

Worthington TA, Brewer SK, Grabowski TB, and Mueller J. In Press. Backcasting the decline of

    a vulnerable Great Plains reproductive ecotype: Identifying threats and conservation

    priorities. *Global Change Biology* DOI: 10.1111/gcb.12329.

Zymonas ND, Propst DL. 2009. A re-analysis of data and critique of Medley et al.—"Simulated

    transport and retention of pelagic fish eggs during an irrigation release in the Pecos River,

    New Mexico". *Journal of Freshwater Ecology* **24**: 671-679. DOI:

    10.1080/02705060.2009.9664347.

Table 1: FRAGSTATS metrics calculated for thirteen US Fish and Wildlife Service fisheries survey sites on the Canadian and North Canadian rivers and the two replacement sites. Initial sites ranked on the metrics total area, shape index and contagion index. Sites in bold represent those selected for egg transport tests. Number in parentheses shows ranking.

Site	River	Total Area (km^2)	% Vegetation	% Shallow Water	% Deep Water	% Sand	Shape Index	Contagion Index	Average Rank
Caddo	Canadian	6.53 (8)	0.00	32.20	47.68	20.12	1.49 (2)	38.54 (2)	4
Wanette	**Canadian**	**14.86 (3)**	**0.00**	**24.75**	**35.18**	**40.07**	**1.41 (6)**	**40.51 (3)**	**4**
Roll	Canadian	6.03 (9)	0.00	45.81	18.61	35.59	1.38 (7)	38.4 (1)	5.67
Bridgeport	**Canadian**	**8.08 (7)**	**0.06**	**10.76**	**40.26**	**48.92**	**1.61 (1)**	**58.44 (12)**	**6.67**
Ada	Canadian	11.57 (5)	0.00	37.43	9.00	53.57	1.34 (13)	42.63 (4)	7.33
Taloga	**Canadian**	**5.68 (10)**	**1.24**	**37.31**	**15.35**	**46.10**	**1.48 (3)**	**49.03 (9)**	**7.33**
Ft. Supply	**N. Canadian**	**0.69 (13)**	**1.40**	**46.22**	**52.38**	**0.00**	**1.47 (4)**	**45.74 (5)**	**7.33**
Calvin	Canadian	17.98 (1)	0.00	20.42	7.20	72.38	1.37 (9)	59.35 (13)	7.67
Norman	**Canadian**	**16.56 (2)**	**4.25**	**44.99**	**11.09**	**39.68**	**1.36 (11)**	**51.76 (10)**	**7.67**
Thomas	Canadian	9.29 (6)	0.00	49.42	5.69	44.89	1.37 (10)	47.69 (7)	7.67
Laverne	**N. Canadian**	**0.69 (12)**	**3.42**	**36.10**	**54.14**	**6.34**	**1.42 (5)**	**46.5 (6)**	**7.67**
Camargo	Canadian	4.47 (11)	3.10	51.94	23.75	21.21	1.37 (8)	48.4 (8)	9
Purcell	**Canadian**	**12.03 (4)**	**1.41**	**45.96**	**9.99**	**42.65**	**1.35 (12)**	**54.32 (11)**	**9**
Norman	Canadian	13.79	7.92	23.20	20.73	48.14	1.44	46.82	
El Reno	N. Canadian	2.15	8.54	7.18	82.46	1.82	1.33	67.66	

Table 2: Median capture time, sampling period length (in parentheses) and transport velocities of egg transport experiments on the Canadian and North Canadian rivers.

Site	Median capture time (h:mm:ss) (95% CI)	Transport velocity (m/s) (95% CI)
Wanette	0:17:12 (0:13:41 - 0:36:27)	0.48 (0.23 - 0.61)
Purcell	0:15:16 (0:12:15 - 0:25:09)	0.55 (0.33 - 0.68)
Norman	0:15:27 (0:12:27 - 0:20:14)	0.54 (0.41 - 0.67)
Bridgeport	0:16:13 (0:14:12 - 0:18:56)	0.51 (0.44 - 0.59)
Taloga	0:20:58 (0:14:46 - 1:06:59)	0.40 (0.12 - 0.56)
El Reno	0:31:57 (0:28:28 - 0:37:43)	0.26 (0.22 - 0.29)
Laverne	1:55:47 (0:55:23 - 4:13:07)	0.07 (0.03 - 0.15)

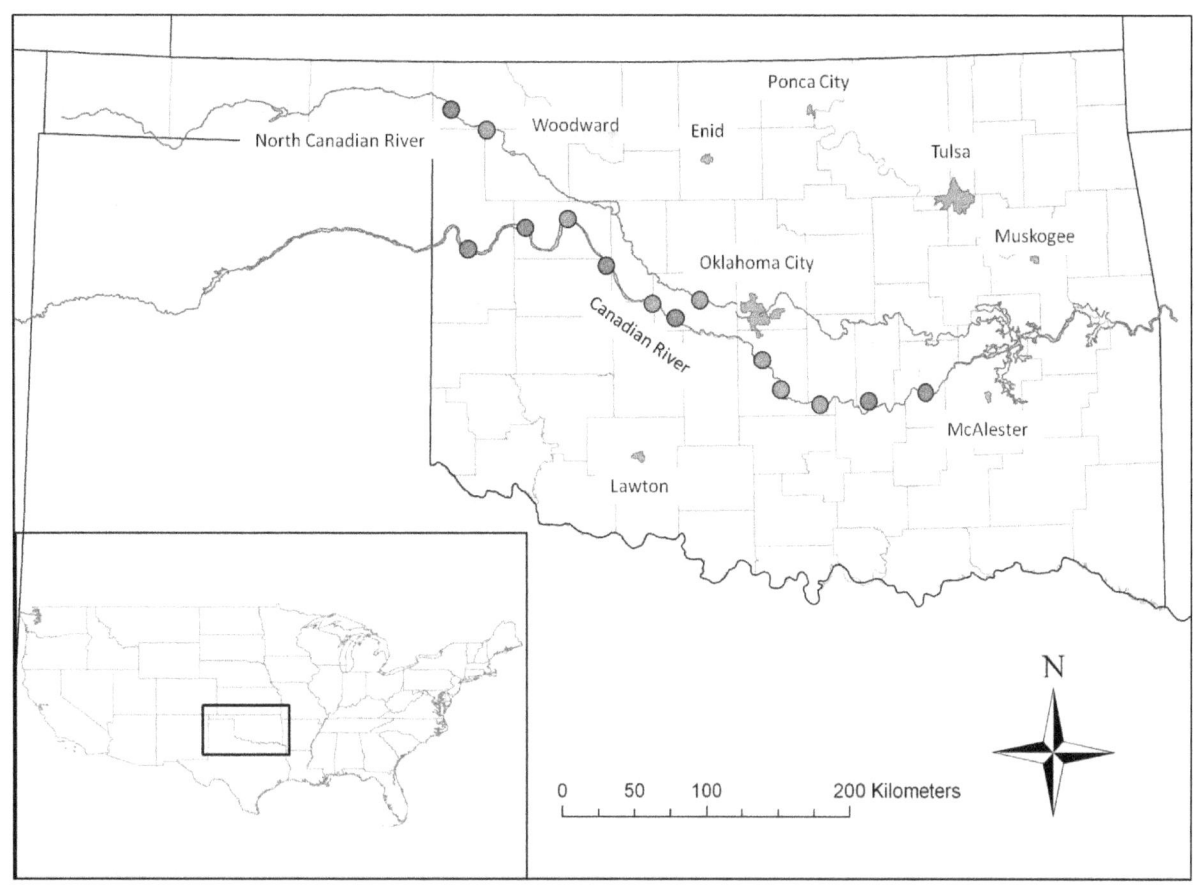

Figure 1: Location of U.S. Fish and Wildlife Service fisheries survey sites, plus replacement site at El Reno. Color denotes sites used only for FRAGSTATs analysis (red) and those used for the egg transport trials (green).

Figure 2: Conversion of aerial photograph into a raster containing four habitat classes.

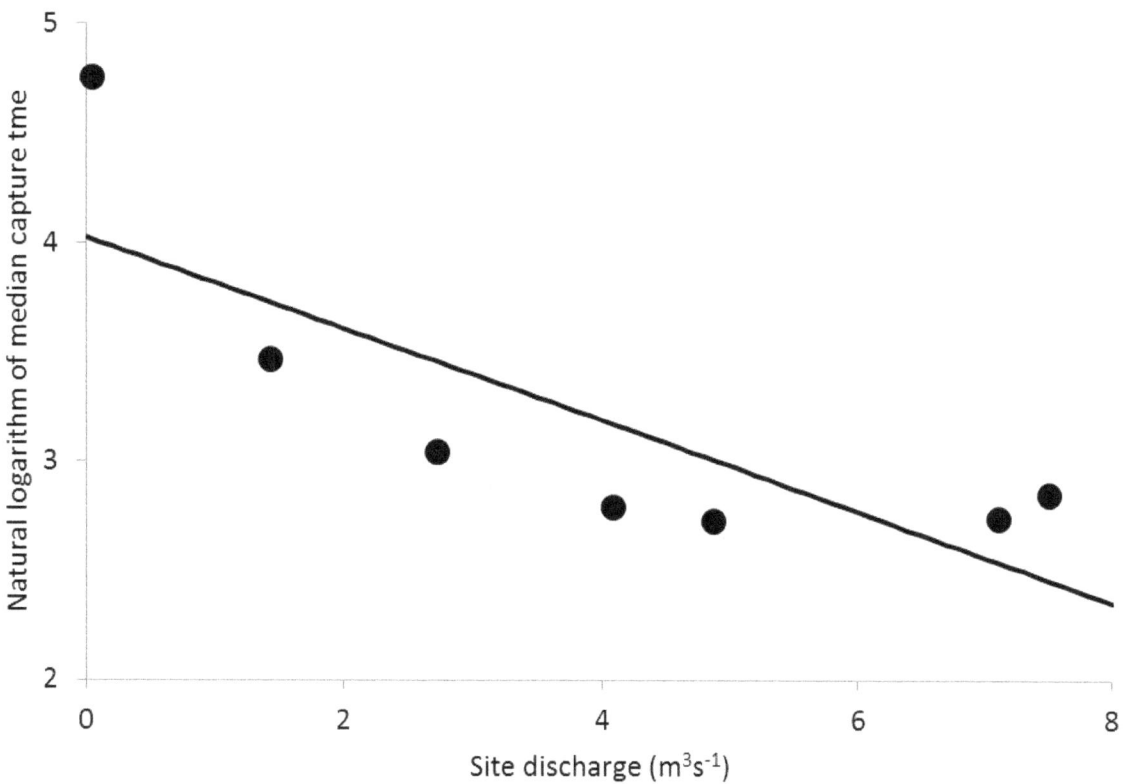

Figure 3: Relationship between site discharge and median transport time for gellan beads at seven sites on the Canadian and North Canadian rivers. Line represents modelled ordinary least squares regression line of best fit, $y = -0.21x_{site\ discharge} + 4.02$; $F_{5,\ 6} = 8.53$, $P = 0.03$, $r^2 = 0.63$.

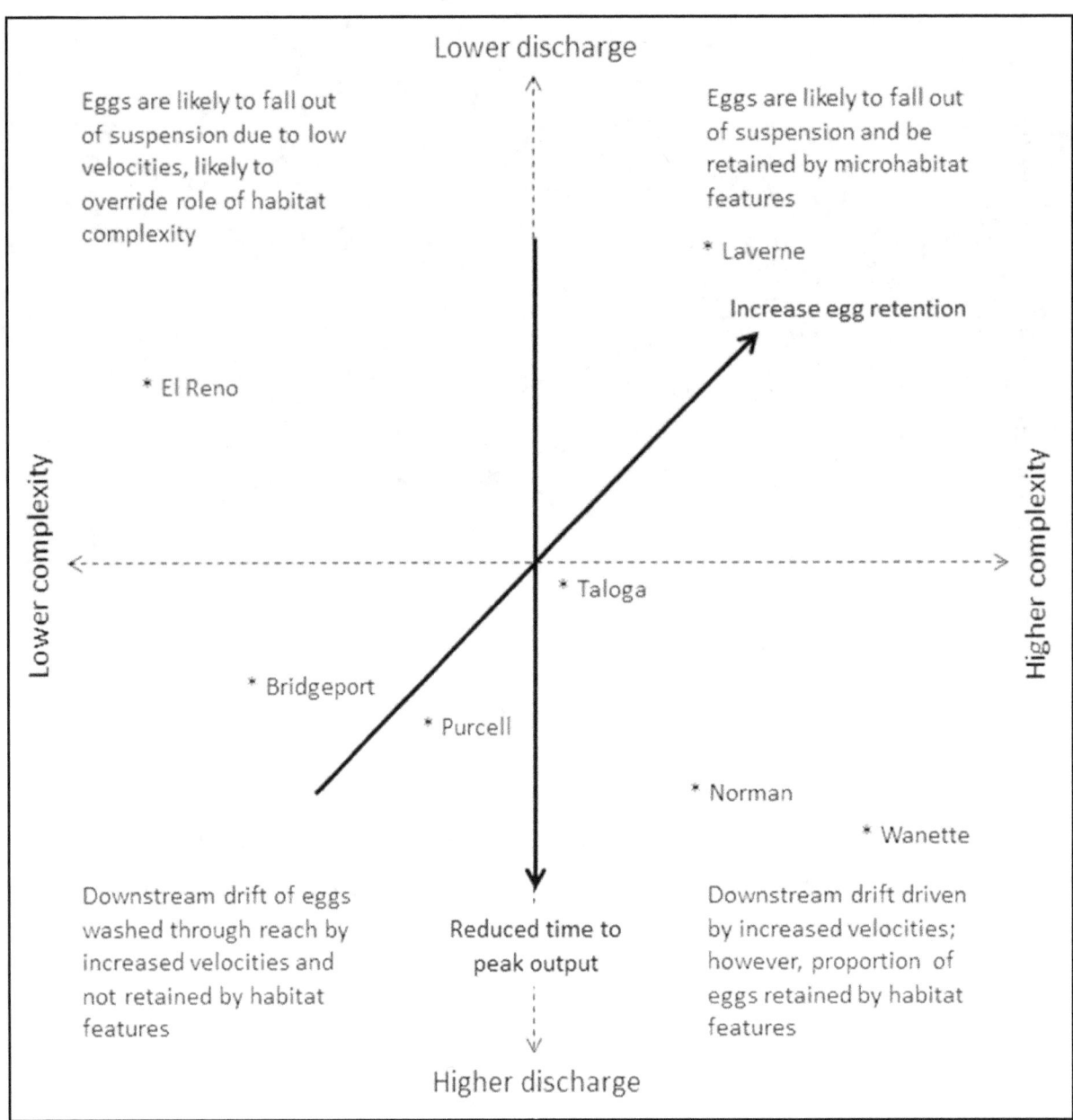

Figure 4: Interaction between discharge and habitat complexity in determining transport speed and retention of passively drifting particles. Position of sampling sites is relative rather than absolute.